JUN 28 2016

DATE DUE

1x 7/16 12·16	
5x (6/17) 8/18	
9x (5/23) 3/25	

BRODART, CO. Cat. No. 23-221

WOOD DALE PUBLIC LIBRARY
DISCARD

Vampires

Katie Griffiths

New York

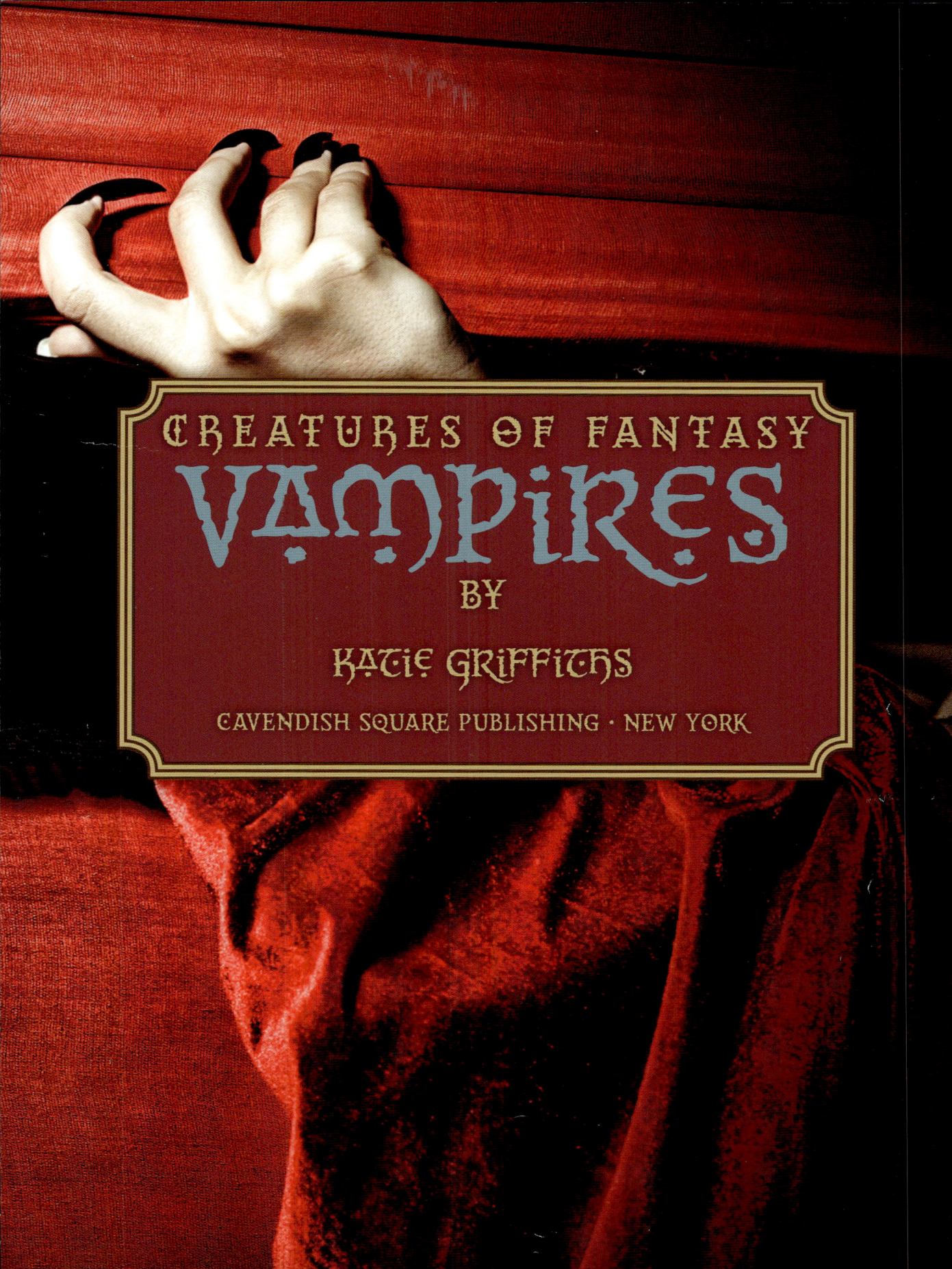

CREATURES OF FANTASY
VAMPIRES

BY

KATIE GRIFFITHS

CAVENDISH SQUARE PUBLISHING · NEW YORK

Published in 2016 by Cavendish Square Publishing, LLC
243 5th Avenue, Suite 136, New York, NY 10016

Copyright © 2016 by Cavendish Square Publishing, LLC

First Edition

No part of this publication may be reproduced, stored in a retrieval system, or transmitted in any form or by any means—electronic, mechanical, photocopying, recording, or otherwise—without the prior permission of the copyright owner. Request for permission should be addressed to Permissions, Cavendish Square Publishing, 243 5th Avenue, Suite 136, New York, NY 10016. Tel (877) 980-4450; fax (877) 980-4454.

Website: cavendishsq.com

This publication represents the opinions and views of the author based on his or her personal experience, knowledge, and research. The information in this book serves as a general guide only. The author and publisher have used their best efforts in preparing this book and disclaim liability rising directly or indirectly from the use and application of this book.

CPSIA Compliance Information: Batch #CW16CSQ

All websites were available and accurate when this book was sent to press.

Library of Congress Cataloging-in-Publication Data

Griffiths, Katie, author.
Vampires / Katie Griffiths.
pages cm. — (Creatures of fantasy)
Includes bibliographical references and index.
ISBN 978-1-5026-0928-1 (hardcover) ISBN 978-1-5026-0929-8 (ebook)
1. Vampires—Juvenile literature. I. Title.
GR830.V3G75 2016
398.21—dc23
2015022187

Editorial Director: David McNamara
Editor: Kristen Susienka
Copy Editor: Nathan Heidelberger
Art Director: Jeffrey Talbot
Designer: Joseph Macri
Senior Production Manager: Jennifer Ryder-Talbot
Production Editor: Renni Johnson
Photo Research: J8 Media

The photographs in this book are used by permission and through the courtesy of: Karen Moskowitz/The Image Bank/Getty Images, cover; Kiselev Andrey Valerevich/Shutterstock.com, 2-3; Hulton Archive/Getty Images, 6, 38; Album/Newscom, 8; Bilwissedition Ltd. & Co. KG/Alamy, 11; File: Queen of the Night BM ME 2003-7-18.1 n01.jpg Unknown artist (Public Domain)/British Museum/©Marie-Lan Nguyen/Wikimedia Commons/CC-BY 2.5, 14; File: Figure of Selene from, "Flora, seu florum." Ferrari 1646 Wellcome L0007609.jpg/Wellcome Library, London. Wellcome Images images@wellcome.ac.uk http://wellcomeimages.org Copyrighted work available under Creative Commons Attribution only licence CC BY 4.0 http://creativecommons.org/licenses/by/4.0/Wikimedia Commons, 18; File: Lady-Lilith.jpg/Dante Gabriel Rossetti (1828–1882)/Bancroft Collection, Wilmington Society of Fine Arts/Wikimedia Commons, 19; Silver Screen Collection/Hulton Archive/Getty Images, 22, 37; PRANA-FILM GMBH, BERLIN/Album/Newscom, 24; File: Friston, Carmilla (Laura in bed).jpg /David Henry Friston, (fl. 1850s to late 1880s)/Wikimedia Commons, 26; JP5\ZOB/WENN.com/Newscom, 28; Pictures from History/Bridgeman Images, 30; Fine Art Images/Heritage Images/Getty Images, 34; DEA/G. DAGLI ORTI/De Agostini/Getty Images, 41, 44; Ionescu Alexandru/Shutterstock.com, 42; Joseph Macri for Cavendish Square, 47; File: Vampire watermelon.jpg/James E. Scarborough (Public Domain) – Wikimedia Commons, 49; © GEFFEN PICTURES/Entertainment Pictures/ZUMAPRESS.com, 52; SNAP/REX/Newscom, 56; UNIMEDIA EUROPE/SND FILMS/Pe/Newscom, 57; ALLOY ENTERTAINMENT/CBS TELEVISION/OUTERBANKS/WARNER BROSS/Album/Newscom, 59.

Printed in the United States of America

CONTENTS

Introduction 7

One
CHILDREN OF THE NIGHT 9

Two
VAMPIRE ORIGINS 15

Three
POWERS AND GIFTS 23

Four
THE COUNT 31

Five
TALES OF FEAR 39

Six
THE WEIRD AND WONDERFUL 45

Seven
MOVING WITH THE TIMES 53

Glossary 60
To Learn More about Vampires 61
Bibliography 62
Index 63
About the Author 64

This 1800s illustration shows a vampire attacking a sleeping girl.

INTRODUCTION

Since the first humans walked the earth, myths and legends have engaged minds and inspired imaginations. Ancient civilizations used stories to explain phenomena in the world around them: the weather, tides, and natural disasters. As different cultures evolved, so too did their stories. From their traditions and observations emerged creatures with powerful abilities, mythical intrigue, and their own origins. Sometimes, different cultures encouraged various manifestations of the same creature. At other times, these creatures and cultures morphed into entirely new beings with greater powers than their predecessors.

Today, societies still celebrate the folklore of their ancestors—on-screen in presentations such as *The Hobbit*, *The Walking Dead*, and *X-Men*; and in stories such as *Harry Potter* and *Twilight*. Some even believe these creatures truly existed and continue to walk the earth as living creatures. Others resign these beings to myth.

In the Creatures of Fantasy series, we celebrate captivating stories of the past from all around the world. Each book focuses on creatures both familiar and unknown: the terrifying ghost, the bloodthirsty vampire, the classic Frankenstein, mischievous goblins, enchanting witches, and the callous zombie. Here their various incarnations throughout history are brought to life. All have their own origins, their own legends, and their own influences on the imagination today. Each story adds a new perspective to the human experience and encourages people to revisit tales of the past in order to understand their presence in the modern age.

I

CHILDREN OF THE NIGHT

*"When other little girls wanted to be ballet dancers,
I kind of wanted to be a vampire."*

ANGELINA JOLIE

WHEN YOU HEAR THE WORD "VAMPIRE" what comes to mind? A sharp-toothed, pale-skinned figure dressed in a cape, hair slicked back and fangs ready to bite? Or a bat flickering in the light of a full moon? What about a coffin or a stake? Throughout the centuries, vampires have come in many shapes, sizes, and symbols. They have been considered real entities by many, while others have simply confined them to horror stories and mythology. Nevertheless, vampire stories have existed for hundreds of years, exciting, frightening, and intriguing many. Today, the vampire remains, but its appearance and purpose has changed, in many instances, for good rather than evil.

Opposite: The new heartthrob: vegetarian vampire Edward Cullen

The Heartthrob Vampire

The year 2005 saw the rise of a new literary heartthrob. Attracted by his killer looks, his morality, and his devotion to his ladylove, thousands of women, young and old, found a new target for their affections. But who was this **paragon** of virtue and smoldering looks? Who had replaced the likes of Mr. Darcy and Heathcliff for a new generation? His name was Edward Cullen, and he was a vampire.

Even fifty years ago it would be hard to imagine that a bloodsucking monster could so easily capture the hearts of a nation. Yet, the vampire has seen a massive reversal in public opinion over the last few decades. It has moved from our blood-soaked nightmares into the light of our fantasies. Unlike the vampires of old, today's creature is a mixture of the divine, the demonic, and the swoon-worthy. However, the journey from repulsive to rock star was not simple or straightforward. The vampire's development and ours have been so closely intertwined that the portrayal of vampires can be seen as a reflection of our own changing fears and social attitudes.

A Very Human Myth

The vampire is a mythological creature that has a **multifaceted** global history. Nearly every single culture has some myth about undead, bloodsucking creatures. Ancient Egyptians told stories of spirits who had been refused entry to the underworld due to improper burial. Once denied, these beings would seek revenge upon the living by drinking their blood. In Celtic Scotland, the Pict tribes warned of the dreaded Dearg-due, literally "Red Blood Sucker." The Dearg-due was created when a young woman who had been forced into marriage killed herself. She was thought to rise again as a blood-hungry demon who would revenge herself upon her father and husband, those responsible for her marriage. Malaysian mythology was even more gruesome. One of their greatest fears was of the Penanggalan. By day she looked like a normal human woman, but by night she sent her disembodied head out into the world in search of blood. She had a particular hunger for babies. It is easy to argue that such stories could only appear in cultures where there was a lack of understanding about medicine and the natural world, but these stories continued into the eighteenth and nineteenth centuries, even as scientific knowledge grew.

Frightened villagers turned to priests for help from vampires.

Tales of vampire activity increased in the closing years of the American Civil War. As soldiers returned home, their families often struggled to recognize their loved ones now scarred physically and mentally from battle. Wandering soldiers, injured and probably experiencing psychological trauma, often prompted tales of vampires lurking in surrounding woodlands. Once again, it was our very human fear of the unknown at the heart of the vampire's continuation.

It is only in more recent times that portrayals of vampires have changed with the rise of the antihero and the supernatural boyfriend. The combination of danger, a heart of gold, and killer abs has been the winning formula behind major literary and screen successes such as *Buffy the Vampire Slayer*, *Twilight*, *True Blood*, and *The Vampire Diaries*. The hapless female victim has become a leading character in her own right and tamed the beast—to a certain extent—into boyfriend material. Yet arguably, fear still lies at the heart of this **trope**. Vampires have now become vehicles to explore teenage anxieties about their own mortality, changing bodies, and adult relationships. While they may not be the subtlest metaphor, vampires have proved extremely effective for authors and filmmakers alike in tackling the teen market.

While these vampires might seem to vary wildly from one story to another, the vampire **canon** does hold some common threads.

The Essential Vampire

The one unifying feature that links all vampire mythology is the draining of some kind of life-force or bodily fluid. In most stories, this first and foremost is blood. In older and more religious cultures, vampires had a particular attraction to the blood of innocents, such as children or virgins. This was usually a means of emphasizing their evil nature. In other societies where a belief in "essence" or "life-force" was present, such as China's belief in chi, vampiric creatures tended instead to consume a person's life force. This could kill them or simply leave them alive but aged, infirm, and weak. It is common in vampire mythology to find tales of beautiful vampire temptresses who leave their male victims drained of their youth and vitality.

Surprisingly, one of the vampire's most noticeable features—its fangs—is a more recent invention. Medieval European mythology rarely mentions enlarged canines, and other cultures at best only note strong or "iron" teeth. Fangs seem to have appeared in vampire stories between the eighteenth and nineteenth centuries. In 1871, Joseph Sheridan Le Fanu published a serial narrative about a female vampire called Carmilla. She is described as having a single fang, "long, thin, pointed … like a needle," that descended over her lip when she was about to feed. It was this story that later influenced the most famous vampire narrative of all time, Bram Stoker's *Dracula*. It was this image of Dracula's teeth, "white as ivory" and "pointed like an animal's," that cemented the vampire's fangs in modern portrayals.

Vampire intelligence has also evolved with time. Ancient folklore has usually portrayed vampires more as a wandering creature with an appetite than a thinking, feeling being. Medieval European folklore described newborn vampires as formless "bags of blood" that required time and feeding to gain rational thought and human form. Similarly, more ancient tales focus on the creature's terrifying hunger rather than their cunning. However, from the eighteenth century onwards, the vampire emerges as possessing a cold, calculating intelligence, using **guile** to befriend victims and allow for slow consumption over a long period.

In fact, the ability of a vampire to control its bloodlust has been a fascinating aspect of its mythology. So often has the vampire appeared to be a strange mix of savage appetites and carefully planned tactics. Its ability to strategize and scheme has varied depending on both the author's intention and the values of the culture that **spawned** it. However, its evolution from creature to sentimental human is an important aspect in vampire lore.

What's in a Name?

There are multiple origins for the word vampire. Some believe that it descends from the Hungarian word for vampire, *vampir*. Different sources argue it is from the Turkish *upior* or *upyr*, which means "witch." Other possibilities include a **derivative** of an Ancient Greek word meaning "to drink"; the Greek *nosophoros*, meaning "plague carrier"; or the Serbian and Serbo-Croatian terms *bamiiup* and *pirati*, which both refer to vampires. One of the most popular theories is that it descended from the Russian term *upir*. This first appeared in 1047 in a document referring to a Russian prince as an *upir lichy*, literally a "wicked vampire."

The first published appearance of "vampire" in the English language was in 1734. It was recorded in a travelogue titled *Travels of Three English Gentlemen*. This word was most likely **derived** from European novels of the period, probably from the French *vampyre* or the German *vampir*.

VAMPIRE ORIGINS

"But first, on earth as Vampire sent,
Thy corse shall from its tomb be rent:
Then ghastly haunt thy native place,
And suck the blood of all thy race"

Lord Byron, "The Giaour"

THE ORIGINS OF THE VAMPIRE MYTH can prove difficult to trace. Many ancient cultures believed in demons and spirits that are now considered precursors to the vampire. Blood drinking was a common occurrence in mythology and in spiritual practices. While today's notion of the vampire originated in southeastern Europe during the early eighteenth century, the mythology that shaped this creature can be traced back much further.

The Demon-Goddess Lilitu

During the Bronze Age, the area known as Mesopotamia (present-day Iraq) was home to advanced civilizations, including the

Opposite: Queen of the Night: the demon goddess Lilitu

Babylonian and Assyrian empires. It was from this basin that one of the most infamous vampiric ancestors emerged—the demon-goddess Lilitu. Her first recorded mention can be found in the literature of the Sumer kingdom, a part of Mesopotamia. The *Epic of Gilgamesh* dates from 2100 BCE and contains the earliest forms of two biblical stories, "Moses in the Bulrushes" and "The Great Flood." It also features the first written story of Lilitu:

> After heaven and Earth had been separated and mankind had been created … a huluppu tree, which had been planted on the bank of the Euphrates and nourished by its waters, was uprooted by the south wind and carried away by the Euphrates. A goddess, who was wandering along the banks, seized the swaying tree and—at the behest of [the gods] Anû and Enlil—brought it to Inanna's garden in Uruk. Inane tended the tree carefully and lovingly; she hoped to have a throne and a bed made for herself from its wood. After ten years, the tree had matured. But in the meantime, she found to her dismay that her hopes could not be fulfilled. Because during that time, a dragon had built its nest at the foot of the tree, the Zu-bird was raising its young in the crown, and the demon Lilitu had built her house in the middle. But Gilgamesh, who had heard of Inanna's plight, came to her rescue. He took his heavy shield, killed the dragon with his gigantic bronze axe … Then the Zu-bird flew into the mountains with its young, while Lilitu, petrified with fear, tore down her house and fled into the wilderness.

Lilitu was later adopted by other cultures, and she would grow from a simple storm demon to the vampiric embodiment of all evil. Not for the first time in male-dominated spiritual literature, she would be held up as a parallel to "good" female characters, like the more nurturing Inanna.

Curse of the Gods

Another origin story for vampires can be found in ancient Greece. Delphi was a famous city inhabited since 1600 BCE and the patron citadel of the Grecian sun god, Apollo. Among the many finds at the city's site, archeologists discovered a set of texts known as the Scriptures of Delphi. These were the recorded prophecies of the Oracle of Delphi. People traveled far and wide to have their futures told by her. According to the texts, Ambrogio was one such man.

In 450 BCE, Ambrogio traveled from Italy to see the Oracle. He was shocked by her short and gruesome prophecy: "The curse. The moon. The blood will run." Confused, Ambrogio spent all night outside the temple pondering what it could mean. At daybreak, a beautiful young woman appeared to tend to the Oracle. She was a priestess of the temple and her name was Selene. Ambrogio began visiting the temple every day to see Selene, and soon they fell in love. He asked her to marry him and come with him to Italy.

During this time, Apollo had been watching and became angered that Ambrogio was wooing one of his priestesses. He cursed Ambrogio so that the touch of the sun would burn his skin, preventing him from meeting Selene the next morning to leave for Italy. In desperation, Ambrogio fled to the underworld to seek the protection of Hades, lord of the dead. Hades agreed to help him, but for a price: Ambrogio's soul. Hades would give him

Ambrogio's doomed lover, Selene, becomes goddess of the moon.

a magical wooden bow, and Ambrogio would use it to kill a swan and offer it as a trophy to the goddess Artemis. Ambrogio would then steal Artemis's silver bow and deliver it to Hades in order to retrieve his soul.

Ambrogio was loath to cross Artemis and used most of his arrows killing swans and writing letters to Selene, but eventually he did manage to steal Artemis's bow. When the goddess realized, she also cursed Ambrogio so that the touch of silver would burn him. Ambrogio was forced to drop the bow before he could deliver it to Hades. He fell to his knees and begged for mercy from the goddess, explaining his situation. In pity, Artemis gave him one last chance. She gifted him with immortality, the speed and strength of a god, and fangs for him to draw blood from animals so as to write letters to Selene.

Selene and Ambrogio were reunited and he explained what had happened. In return for her gifts, the couple agreed to solely worship Artemis. As a virgin goddess, she required her followers to also be chaste, and thus the couple was never allowed to have a child or even to kiss. As the years went by, Selene grew older and older, and soon she was close to death. Ambrogio bargained with Artemis and she offered one last deal. Ambrogio was permitted to touch Selene just once and drink her blood. The act would kill her mortal body but give her everlasting life. After Ambrogio had finished, Selene's spirit rose into the night sky and she became the goddess of the moon.

The Lady Lilith

The First Wife of Adam

During the Middle Ages, there was another woman held up as an example of the connection between monstrosity and bad female behavior. Her name was Lilith, a character from Jewish mythology. In the *Alphabet of Ben Sira*, the story of creation sees Lilith as the first wife of Adam. She is created from the same clay as Adam rather than from his rib, as later happened with Eve. She refuses to be subservient to Adam and eventually leaves the Garden of Eden. She is later cursed to spend the night in vampire form as punishment. The connection between "bad" female behavior and monstrosity continued as her mythology developed. In her stories, she would appear in two forms. When faced with a man, Lilith became an evil seductress or **succubus** and drained men of their vitality. When confronted with a woman, she would transform into a demonic mother figure, harming pregnant women and stealing newborns. Time and again, her carnivorous desire for blood was emphasized. In his book *Lilith: The First Eve*, scholar Sigmund Hurwitz notes: "She is always poised to kill the child so that she can drink its blood and suck the marrow from its bones. This aspect of Lilith is already conveyed in early texts, in which she is called 'the strangler.'"

Vampire Fever

The modern image of the classic vampire—an undead, bloodsucking corpse—developed in the late seventeenth and early eighteenth centuries. The first recorded sightings began in 1672 from the region of Istria in present-day Croatia. Jure Grando, a former peasant who had died some years before, was reported to be harassing his widow and attacking other villagers. He is referred to as a *štrigun,* a local word meaning a "vampire-warlock." This was the first case in history where a real person had been described as a vampire in government documents. These tales later traveled to Germany and England where they were embellished and popularized.

The eighteenth century is commonly known as the Age of Enlightenment, promoting the values of reason, critical thinking, and order. Yet despite this, it was a period that saw belief in vampires rise dramatically, resulting in mass hysteria and even public executions. In Eastern Europe, there was a rash of stakings, beheadings, and grave diggings. These processes were meant to identify and kill potential vampires. There were two particularly famous cases in Serbia involving a peasant named Petar Blagojevich and a former soldier named Arnold Paole. After he had been buried, Blagojevich allegedly returned home to his family, asking for food. His son refused and was found dead the next day. Blagojevich is also thought to have attacked some neighbors who had died from blood loss. Paole, on the other hand, was believed to have been attacked by a vampire some years before, and after his death, he was thought to have returned to feed on his neighbors.

Eventually, mass hysteria escalated across Europe. There were reports of blood oozing from dead bodies. Sometimes wounds thought to have come from a vampire would appear on a body. Many believed these signs to indicate a vampire. Sometimes people killed others who showed these signs. Other times, people thought that if their loved ones were buried with these marks on them they would emerge from their graves as vampires and attack others, continuing the cycle. People became fearful of burying the dead. There were many instances where rural communities performed rituals to prevent corpses from becoming vampires. For example, people dug up local cemeteries and either decapitated or burned bodies inside graves to ensure they could not return as vampires. The panic only subsided when Austria finally stepped in. Empress Maria Theresa of Austria sent her personal physician, Gerard van Swieten, to investigate claims of vampire activities. He eventually concluded vampires did not exist and the empress passed laws prohibiting the opening of graves and desecration of bodies. However, by this time the vampire was a fixed entity in the European mind and continued to appear in the region's literature and art.

Waking the Dead

One example of vampirism in ancient mythology can be found in Ancient Egypt, where rituals surrounding death were sacred and extremely complex. For the Egyptians, there were very real consequences for an incorrect or incomplete burial. According to the Egyptian Book of the Dead, there are five parts to the soul: the *ib* (heart), *sheut* (shadow), *ren* (name), *ba* (personality), and *ka* (vital spark). The Egyptians believed it was the ka that made the difference between a living and a dead person, and death could only occur once the ka had left the body. It was breathed into the body upon the moment of birth and was sustained through food and drink. However, ka could linger in the body after death and thus had to be appeased through offerings of food and drink. Family members would present food at the tombs of their relations and ancestors. The *kau* (essence) of the food would be consumed but not the physical aspect. If the family was negligent or made insufficient offerings, the dead would go out into the world and seek revenge by drinking the blood of the living.

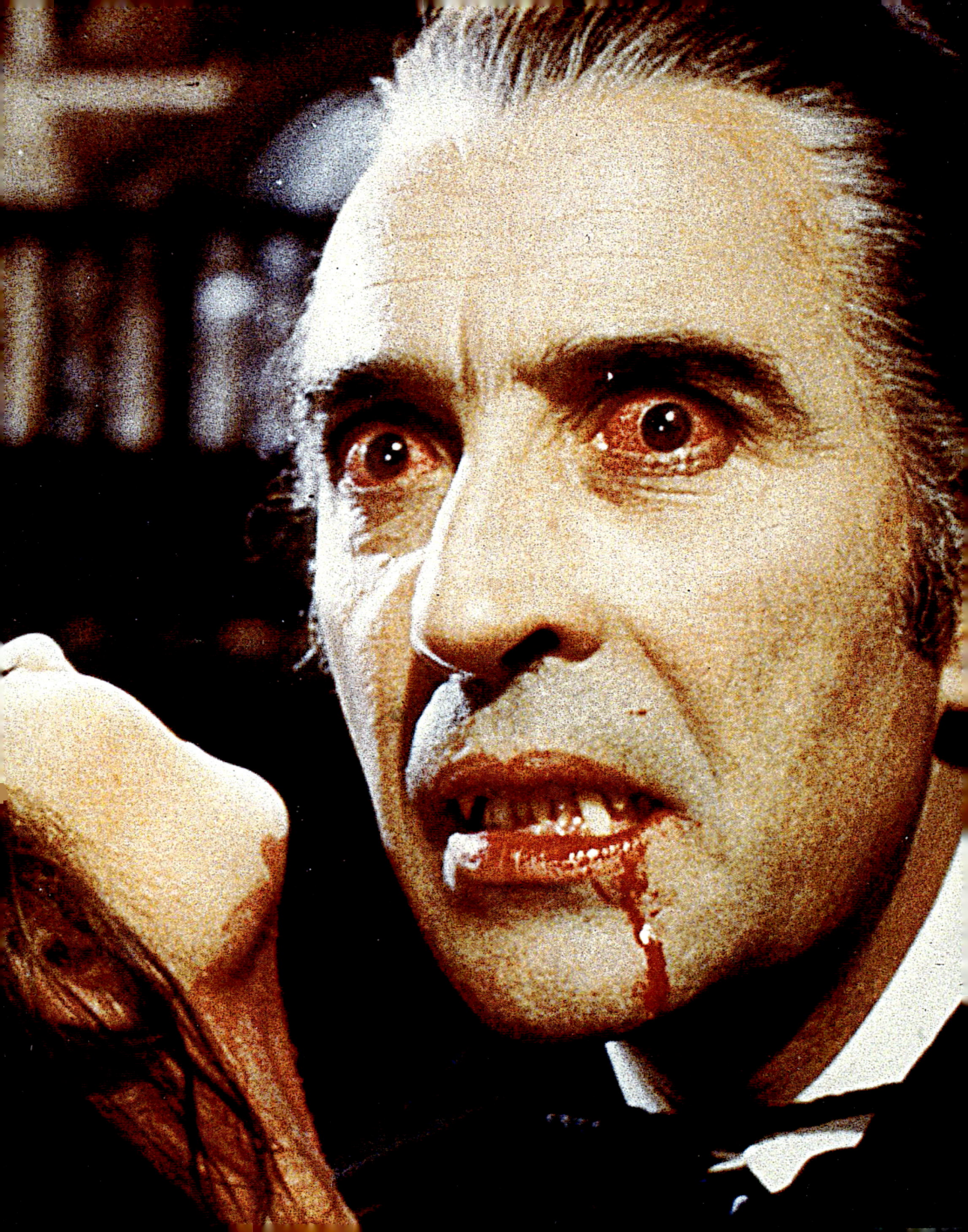

3

POWERS AND GIFTS

"There is no such creature as 'The Vampire'; there are only vampires."

NINA AUERBACH, *OUR VAMPIRES, OURSELVES*

IT CAN SOMETIMES APPEAR THAT VAMPIRES have more powers than Superman. They can fly, shape-shift, cast spells, sparkle—the list goes on. However, there are a few "standard" vampire powers that have evolved into vampire lore today. Each author or storyteller adds their own embellishment to the vampire trope, and vampiric attributes are often adapted to suit the character and society of origin.

JUST A BITE

The one connecting factor that unites all vampires is the ability to gain energy through feeding on blood. The practice of hematophagy (bloodsucking) allows them to regenerate wounds and sustain

Opposite: English actor Christopher Lee as the Count in Dracula AD *(1972).*

living flesh. Vampires are technically dead, and without fresh blood their bodies will quickly decay. Since vampires do not have active digestive systems, they are unable to digest food and drink. Instead, blood is ingested and absorbed directly into the bloodstream. It is believed that a vampire must feed at least a couple times a week in order to stay strong, and more is needed if the creature has been injured seriously. Some folklore has suggested that the older a vampire becomes, the less blood it requires to stay strong. Often in vampire tales, the older a vampire is, the more powerful and "demonic" it becomes.

A scene from *Nosferatu*, featuring Count Orlok, one of history's most famous film vampires.

Eye of the Tiger

Whether the vampire is feeding or defending itself, the creature has more or less a smorgasbord of physical tools for any task. In more typical tales, vampires are characterized by superhuman strength, physical ability, and a magnified sense of smell and vision. Bram Stoker's Dracula is frequently described as having "the strength of twenty men." In the wildly successfully *Twilight*, the main character, Bella, researches vampire folklore and discovers one particular species, the Slovakian *nelapsi*, who are thought to be "so strong and fast [that they] could massacre an entire village in the single hour after midnight." In addition, the vampires of the Twilight series have such amazing strength and skill that they can only play outdoor games during thunderstorms, the reason being that no one else will be outside to see their incredible speed and that the thunderclaps mask the deafening sounds the vampires make when slamming into each other during the game.

Modern-day TV shows such as *Buffy the Vampire Slayer*, *The Vampire Diaries*, and *True Blood* are filled with acrobatic vampires who move in blurs, throw each other through solid walls, and can hear a human's heartbeat from fifty paces away. In spite of this violence, today's vampires are still incredibly graceful. Gracefulness is often one of their most attractive qualities. Vampires are often described in terms of their "sleekness" or "catlike" movements. They have become metaphorical tigers, beautiful yet deadly, graceful but ferocious.

Vampires in today's films, books, and television shows have become increasingly self-mocking and self-referential when discussing their abilities. For instance, in the first season of *The Vampire Diaries*, lead vampire Damon discusses vampire life with the then-human Caroline. She has a copy of the book *Breaking Dawn* from the Twilight series. When he reads about the vampires in this book, Damon jokes that, unlike the vampires in the book, he does not sparkle in the sun. Writers and directors of these shows often play with the current popularity of the vampire genre, either to promote their vampires as the "true" vampires or simply to poke fun at the increasing varieties of powers and talents.

That Old Black Magic

Some vampires possess more fantastic abilities. Stoker's Dracula, for example, frequently creeps upon his victims by turning himself into mist. Alone in her bedroom, the heroine, Mina, notices outside the window "a thin streak of white mist, that crept with almost imperceptible slowness across the grass towards the house [and] seemed to have a **sentience** and a vitality of its own." Literature of this period often used weather to convey inner turmoil or impending doom. However, in the hands of vampires it became far more sinister. Mina soon realizes that the mist—Dracula in disguise—has "poured" itself into her room despite the locked window. Nowhere is safe from a thing that can so easily change its physical state.

This illustration from 1872 shows vampire Carmilla surprising character Laura at night.

In addition, the vampire has more than air in its transformation arsenal. It is not uncommon in vampire folklore for the creature to turn into a bat, a dog, or sometimes a wolf. In the case of Joseph Sheridan Le Fanu's infamous Carmilla, she appears in beast-state as a "sooty-black animal that resembled a monstrous cat." In fact, Carmilla is compared to an animal even when in human form. Her movements have "the lithe restlessness of a beast in a cage" and her crypt where she returns to her coffin to sleep is described as "the lair of [a] beast."

Writers have often played on the connection between vampires and animals.

In some tales, vampires can control beasts, overriding their will, and other times they seem to share a more brotherly connection, exhibiting similar characteristics and behaviors. This is often closely related to whether the writer wishes to portray vampires as mostly human or mostly creature. The more animalistic the vampire, the less sympathy a writer or speaker tends to have towards their characters.

Time, the invention of the film industry, and the rise in vampire fiction for teens has further added to this list. Their physical abilities have developed into flying and levitation. Their primitive magic has expanded to include the power to become invisible, travel through time, and cast spells. Some can even withstand sunlight with no more protection than a great haircut.

Lastly, vampires are well known for their beauty sleep inside coffins. The use of coffins appears to date back to the eighteenth century. Villagers would open coffins during the day in order to "catch" a powerless vampire. Literature and film have played with these conventions. In Bram Stoker's *Dracula*, the title character uses his coffin to cross the sea to England; however, it must first be packed with the earth of his home country. More modern adaptations have focused less on the need for coffins and more on a vampire's need for a resting place in complete darkness during the day.

These weapons and charms were believed to help kill or weaken vampires.

Strangeness and Charms

Apotropaics or apotropaic magic were items or spells traditionally believed to protect people from evil creatures and spirits. The word comes from the Greek *apotrepein*, meaning "to ward off." Most commonly, apotropaics come in the form of amulets or in gestures such as crossing your fingers or knocking on wood. In older times, apotropaics were used to ward off vampires and were commonly found in vampire folklore. People used items such as garlic, wild rose and hawthorn plant branches, and mustard seeds. After the rise of Christianity in Europe during the Middle Ages, these grew to include crucifixes, rosaries, and holy water. It was believed that vampires could not walk on consecrated grounds—for example, those of churches or temples—or cross running water. Less well-known apotropaics include mirrors. These were placed on doors facing outward, as it was believed that vampires did not have reflections due to their lack of a soul. The oldest of all apotropaic magic are thresholds. A characteristic that has not changed through vampire mythology is their inability to enter a house without the owner's invitation. Thus the owner's refusal of an invite was believed to be the strongest way to protect a home.

4

THE COUNT

"The prince of vampires is Bram Stoker's Dracula, round whom centres probably the greatest horror tale of modern times."

DEVENDRA VARMA, *THE GOTHIC FLAME*, 1966

THE LEADING LIGHT OF ALL VAMPIRE literature is surely Count Dracula himself. Appearing in books, films, art, and more, the character has probably had a stronger influence upon the representation of vampires than any other character from the genre.

The character first appeared in Bram Stoker's gothic horror novel, *Dracula*. The novel tells the story of the vampire Count Dracula's attempt to move from his home in Transylvania to England. He goes in search of new blood and to create new vampire brides, but he soon meets his match in the form of a group of young men and women led by vampire hunter Professor Van Helsing. Since its publication in 1897, the book has never

Opposite: The cover of Bram Stoker's *Dracula*, 1916 edition

gone out of print and has spawned numerous television, film, and radio adaptations and spoofs.

The Prince of Darkness

Dracula is a story that has **crystallized** the modern image of the vampire in many ways, both in his physical appearance and the use of vampirism as a vehicle to explore social issues.

Though not the first of his kind, Stoker's vampire was the epitome of the nineteenth-century "noble vampire," a vampire who appears to be part of upper-class society. Dracula dresses in fine clothes, lives in a stately castle, and in both his education and mannerisms he is clearly a member of the **aristocracy**. His appearance in particular has stuck in the public imagination. In *Dracula in the Dark: The Dracula Film Adaptations*, scholar James Holte argues that "the figure of Stoker's most famous vampire, complete with cape, evening dress, and fangs, is one the most widely recognized visual symbols in the world." This is true. We need only glimpse a figure with these characteristics to immediately understand the reference. This reference has appeared in a number of places, including on a cereal box—Count Chocula.

Similarly, Count Dracula emphasized wealth and intelligence in the vampire persona. Prior to the nineteenth century, vampires had been largely beasts of appetite. They were usually peasants who had become vampires due to incorrect burial. They were considered more animal than anything, and displayed little more than the cunning of a predator. Dracula was a move away from this, described as possessing "stately" grace and "white and fine" hands. He is "clever," "subtle," and "resourceful." Though the other characters describe him time and again as a "creature" in order to emphasize his lack of humanity, Professor Van Helsing and his team must attempt to kill him through more intelligent methods rather than an all-out animal hunt. Dracula's ability to strategize and manipulate humans can never be underestimated, and ultimately it requires a group of mentally strong and highly religious humans to bring down just one vampire.

The novel also greatly reflects a number of social issues that consumed its contemporary society. Concerns over invasion and the British Empire were common during the Victorian period. It was at this point in history when the British Empire was at its largest. While this was a point of pride for many Victorians, it was also a deep concern. While colonies mutinied abroad, conservative Victorian values seemed to be in decline on the home front. New scientific knowledge, such as Charles Darwin's *On the Origins of Species*, had led to a rapid decline in Christian belief. Political movements such as the **suffragettes** were causing some women to turn away from traditional family structures and roles. The rise in diseases such as tuberculosis and syphilis inflamed public concern over infections. Novels of this period were often greatly riddled with these themes and would explore them using different methods—the use of fantasy, science fiction, and gothic horror were favorites.

During the 1880s and 1890s, many famous authors wrote tales in which fantastical creatures invaded the British Empire. To Stoker's contemporary readers, *Dracula* would have been seen as a typical adventure story of its time, though Stoker was praised for his skill.

Under the Influence

Scholar Elizabeth Signorotti sees Dracula not as the beginning of a new kind of vampire but rather as its completed form. She argues: "Of the vampire tales to date, Bram Stoker's *Dracula* has unquestionably become the most popular and the most critically examined. It constitutes, however, the culmination of a series of nineteenth-century vampire tales that have been overshadowed by Stoker's 1897 novel." It is true. Dracula, despite his many talents, did not appear out of thin air. He was a creation that owed a large debt to history. Stoker is believed to have been influenced by other figures, both historical and fictional, from his own century and previous ones.

Historically, many researchers believe that the two greatest inspirations for the character of Count Dracula were the Romanian prince Vlad Tepes and the lesser-known Hungarian countess Erzsébet Báthory.

Portrait of Vlad Tepes

Vlad Tepes, known by his nickname Dracula, lived during the fifteenth century. He was born and raised in Transylvania but ruled over southern Romania. His father, Dracul, was a powerful and feared leader. In 1431, the Holy Roman Emperor made Dracul a member of the Order of the Dragon, a semi-military organization that was dedicated to fighting Turkish **infidels**. *Dracul* is a Romanian word for "dragon," but it can also mean "devil." Dracul soon added the image of the dragon to his military banner, but suspicious peasants took this to be a sign he was in league with the devil. His son Vlad's nickname, Dracula, meant "son of the dragon" or possibly "son of the devil."

Vlad soon followed his father's warlike example and gained a new nickname, Vlad the Impaler. In their book *In Search of Dracula*, writers Raymond T. McNally and Radu Florescu note:

> He was known mostly for the amount of blood he indiscriminately spilled, not only the blood of the infidel Turks—which, by the standards of the time, would make him a hero—but that of Germans, Romanians, Hungarians, and other Christians. His ingenious mind devised all kinds of tortures, both physical and mental, and his favorite way of imposing death earned him the name "the Impaler."

There is some disagreement amongst scholars as to whether Stoker's Count Dracula is supposed to be the Romanian prince Dracula or not. Some have argued Stoker merely took the name after he had written his book to make his character sound more authentic, whilst others point to historic references in the novel as proof of Stoker's intentional casting of Prince Dracula as a character.

Another possible inspiration for the character was Hungarian countess Erzsébet Báthory. She lived during the late sixteenth and seventeenth centuries and was accused of torturing and killing hundreds of girls between 1585 and 1610. The exact number is unknown. The influence of her family saved her from facing trial. Much like the Romanian Prince Vlad, her story quickly became part of national folklore, and it was widely rumored that she bathed in the blood of her victims to retain her youthful beauty. She has been nicknamed "The Blood Countess" and "Countess Dracula."

Dracula also had various literary influences. The nineteenth century saw the rise of the "noble" vampire—a creature as rich and dashing as it was dangerous. Until this time, vampires were simply peasants who had transformed due to incorrect burials, **impiety**, or merely bad luck. Yet in 1819, a man called John Polidori published *The Vampyre*, a tale of a young aristocratic man who makes friends with a mysterious nobleman. The man soon discovers his new friend is seducing and feeding on young aristocratic women from their social circle. Polidori was actually the physician to the famous British poet Lord Byron and, in fact, based his vampiric nobleman on his patient. With this novel, the vampire moved from something disgusting and monstrous to a creature that was dangerous and murderous, but also darkly desirable.

The other most notable literary influence was that of Joseph Sheridan Le Fanu's 1872 gothic novella *Carmilla*. The story tells of the young noblewoman Laura who befriends another young noblewoman, Carmilla. They become fast friends, though Laura becomes increasingly confused by her friend's strange behavior. It is later discovered that Carmilla is a centuries-old vampire who has been feeding on Laura. Many scholars have argued that the character of Carmilla was the prototype for the modern female vampire—beautiful, dangerous, and manipulative. Le Fanu's novella is also credited with gifting the vampire legend with fangs. Previous vampires had never been described with fangs, but, as mentioned earlier, Carmilla is described as possessing one single fang that protrudes over her lip when she is hungry or under attack.

The Children of the Night

It is clear that Dracula continues be a cultural icon and to influence the depiction of vampires today. Though Stoker's *Dracula* was popular with its contemporary audience, it was not until the advent of the silver screen that the character gained legendary status. As of 2014, Dracula has been featured in a major role in over five hundred films. Popular adaptations include the 1931 *Dracula* starring Bela Lugosi in his career-defining role as Count Dracula, *Nosferatu* (1922), and *Dracula Untold* (2014). *Nosferatu's* director, F. W. Murnau, was forced to change the villain's name to Count Orlok after Stoker's widow refused to give permission.

Bela Lugosi as Dracula and Frances Dade as Lucy in *Dracula* (1931)

The Chinese Jiangshi

In Chinese mythology, vampires and zombies collide in the form of the *jiangshi*. It is a type of reanimated corpse, typically described as wearing official garments from the Qing dynasty (1644–1912). It kills its victims to absorb their chi, or life essence, and only appears at night. A jiangshi spends the daylight hours resting in a coffin or a dark cave. It moves around by hopping with its arms outstretched. There are believed to be several possible causes for the creation of a jiangshi. They can be created by the use of magic to raise the dead, the demonic possession of a dead body, or the corpse's absorption of enough *yang qi* (life essence) to return it to life. The most common method is through the failure of a person's soul to leave the body due to improper death, suicide, or a wish for vengeance. In more modern depictions, a person can be turned into a jiangshi through being attacked by the creature and becoming infected with the "jiangshi virus"—much like zombies and werewolves.

TALES OF FEAR

*"Our monsters are defined by our culture
—show me what you fear and I will show you what you are."*
KEITH SCOTT, "BLOOD, BODIES, BOOKS:
KIM NEWMAN AND THE VAMPIRE AS A CULTURAL TEXT"

SINCE THEIR FIRST CREATION, VAMPIRES have been used to tell stories, to put our darkest fears into something tangible, something that has rules and is governed by some kind of law, even if that law is not man-made. Critic Kevin Scott argues that "human beings are the storytelling species who make sense of the world around us by articulating experience through forms and frameworks of accepted narrative structure." By this he meant that humans have a need to talk about their lives and how they experience the world. However, in order for us to communicate as a species, we must have certain storylines and characters that everyone recognizes and understands. The vampire is but one of these shared narratives.

Opposite: Dieter Eppler as the Vampire in *Curse of the Blood Ghouls* (1962)

Though each generation has created its own version of the vampire, the themes that vampires are used to explore remain the same—love, death, and power. At their deepest heart, all fears can be traced back to these key themes.

Disease and Death

The connection between vampires and death, while seemingly obvious, is still very complex. Historically, vampire mythology was used to explain the spread of disease and plague. Before science could explain changes in weather conditions or an infectious outbreak, people were forced to invent reasons for unexplainable deaths or crop failures within a community. In 2009, archaeologists discovered a sixteenth-century female skull with a rock wedged in its mouth buried near the remains of plague victims. This **obstruction** of the mouth was used on suspected vampires and was believed during this time to prevent the creature from feeding on the bodies of plague victims or attacking the living. Female vampires were often blamed for the spread of the bubonic plague throughout Europe. Similarly, during the medieval period, babies with birth defects or abnormalities were also believed to be vampires or demons. Lack of medical knowledge meant that ignorance often gave way to fear, and the character of the vampire stepped in to fill the void. The idea that disease and sudden deaths were being caused by some being—no matter how outlandish or extraordinary—was an easier story for poorly educated people, who had often never left the village they were born in, to understand.

The characteristics of vampires, such as their coffin beds, were also probably due to a lack of medical and scientific knowledge. Thanks to modern developments, previous gravedigger and mortician reports of "rising" corpses have been discovered to be part of the decomposition process, where the escaping gases can make a body appear to be moving. Likewise, there were often reports of graves being unearthed and their occupants being found with blood around the mouth, thus proving their vampire status. It is now known that the decomposition of the intestines can create bloating, forcing blood up to the mouth and creating the impression of bloodsucking evidence.

Repression and Attraction

Another key factor of vampire tales is attraction. Modern and old stories are full of creatures that pull us toward them against our better judgment. They are beautiful and exciting—even as we fear them, we want to know them more. Our ability, or inability, to control our desires has been explored using vampires time and time again.

This nineteenth-century illustration shows a mother and her children begging.

The nineteenth century was the first age of vampire literature. For a long time, one of the most dangerous things men and women could do was to have relations outside of marriage. Any woman who fell pregnant without the protection of a husband was seen as a threat to social order. She and her children would have no money to live on, often nowhere to live, and would possibly be refused shelter and employment due to the mother's lack of "moral values." Being rejected by society would have repercussions on both the woman and her children for the rest of their lives. Men also faced punishments, though not as severe. A man who could not prove his children had been born from a lawful marriage would risk his family's wealth and estate. The law often prevented children born out of wedlock from inheriting family property and wealth, reducing them to a life of poverty. Order was believed to be the most important value of society. Families were the bedrock of that order. Thus, order was dictated by marriage, and marriage was controlled to ensure that family lines were continued and property was safeguarded. The biggest threat to this order was the individual's desires. If a single person could simply have relations with anyone, there would be no way to ensure social security. The vampire, at this time, embodied that threat. It was a danger that prompted both fear and attraction—as danger has always done.

The Politics of Tyranny

Vampires also appear in our narrative of politics and class struggle. For years, the creature has been used as a metaphor for manipulative upper classes "feeding" on the strength of the lower classes. Classic literary vampires have always been associated with the aristocracy—*Count* Dracula, *Countess* Carmilla, and *Lord* Ruthven from Polidori's *The Vampyre* are a few examples.

Dracula's castle in Romania

The connection between feeding and absorbing the strength of a victim can be traced back to ancient times. Many societies believed that drinking another's blood would allow the drinker to take on the sacrifice's vitality or essence. For example, the blood of a warrior would make you stronger, or wolf's blood could make you more cunning. Modern ethics have now ruled out this practice as barbaric; however, it still holds great metaphoric significance. Even today, some religions have ceremonies where worshippers symbolically drink a god's blood, such as at Catholic communion.

Real-Life Vampires

In today's society, there are people who identify themselves as vampires. They come from a wide variety of backgrounds, and because they are unwilling to reveal themselves publicly, their exact number in unknown. They broadly fall into two categories: those who identify as "sanguine" vampires, and those who identify themselves as "pranic." Sanguine vampires believe they need to drink human or animal blood to stay strong. Pranic vampires say they feed off the energy of other humans, rather than on physical blood. The word "pranic" comes from the Hindu concept of *prana*, or energy. Some groups have claimed that their practices are based on a "vampire-donor" relationship of mutual respect and pointed out that any physical or psychic feeding hinges on consent. However, doctors and psychologists cite multiple cases where a person's belief in their vampiric nature has resulted in suicide or murder.

THE WEIRD AND WONDERFUL

"In Ghat they believe in vampire watermelons, although folklore is silent about what they believe about vampire watermelons. Possibly they suck back."

TERRY PRATCHETT, *CARPE JUGULUM*

WHILE VAMPIRE FOLKLORE CAN BE at turns both bizarre and shocking, there can still be stranger happenings found on its outskirts. Key aspects of vampire mythology can be traced back to the religious beliefs of ancient civilization, immortal concerns over health and the home, and the use of rituals to guard against the forces of darkness.

Bloodthirsty Deities

If newspapers and mass media are to be believed, modern society has become an increasingly violent place. This alleged rise in violence is often attributed to video games, rap music, or action films. While these may account for some events, death and

Opposite: A wood statute of the Egyptian lioness goddess Sekhmet

destruction has always been part of human civilization. Today many people are both terrified and fascinated by it, and ancient societies were no different.

In Ancient Egypt, Sekhmet was the lion-headed goddess of war, vengeance, menstruation, and medicine. Her followers were connected by one thing: blood. She was often shown wearing a blood-red dress, and was also known as the "Lady of Slaughter" and "She Who **Mauls**." In one story, her father, Ra, king of the gods, sends her to Earth to destroy the humans who have been conspiring against him. However, Sekhmet quickly becomes mad with bloodlust and almost destroys the whole of humanity. To calm her fury, Ra pours beer that has been dyed red on the fields. Believing it to be blood, Sekhmet drinks the beer and soon falls asleep drunk. When she awakes, her bloodlust has dissipated and she returns to her father.

Ancient India channeled its obsession with mortality and violence through the goddess Kali. She represented time, death, and destruction, and she was often depicted fanged, garlanded with skulls, and dripping blood. The Thuggee cult worshipped her and built her temples close to cremation grounds. Her most famous feat was in battle with a demon called Raktavija (Blood Seed). He was able to reproduce himself from a single drop of blood. Every time Kali cut him, another demon was created. She eventually **thwarted** him by drinking every last drop of blood from his body.

Cousins of the Vampire

Vampire characteristics get increasingly strange as we look outside of mainstream fiction and folklore. While they still reflect concerns over death, blood loss, and violence, each culture has adapted them to suit their surroundings.

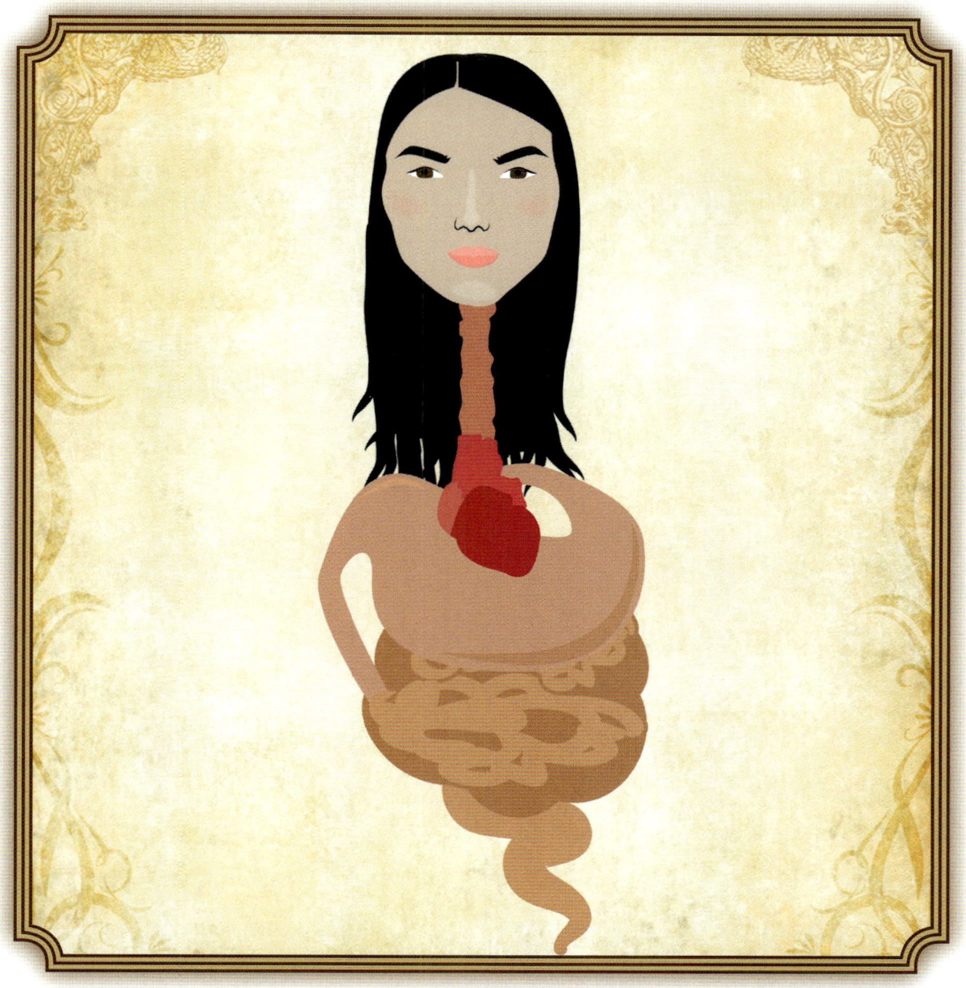

An illustration of Malaysia's Penanggalan, also known as the Southeast Asian Vampire

As previously mentioned, in Malaysia the vampire finds its cousin in the Penanggalan. By day, it looks like a beautiful woman; however, at night her head detaches and goes flying into the night while her stomach and insides dangle below. A Penanggalan is believed to be created when a midwife breaks a pact she has made with the devil to gain supernatural power. Once the pact is broken she is forever cursed. Her victims are traditionally pregnant women or children. When a woman is in labor, the Penanggalan will perch on the roof screeching before inserting a long, invisible tongue into the house to drink the blood of the new mother. The victim will then contract a fatal **wasting** disease. Once the Penanggalan returns home, she must shrink her organs in vinegar to fit them back into her body.

One possible origin of the Penanggalan is believed to be an unfortunate priestess. Stories say that one day she was taking a ritual bath in vinegar. While bathing and deeply meditating, a man entered the room without warning and startled her. The priestess was so shocked that she jerked her head up quickly, severing it from her body. Enraged, the priestess's head flew after the man, leaving her body behind in the bath of vinegar. It is believed that even in the daytime a Penanggalan can be differentiated from an ordinary woman by the odor of vinegar.

Bizarre vampire folklore doesn't end there. One legend from the Balkans tells of vampire fruit! Gypsy communities in Kosovo have told folktales of vampire pumpkins and watermelons. Watermelons that have begun to rot often display red marks on their skin. To a believer in vampires, this was thought to be a sign that the fruit had been feeding on blood. It was believed that leaving the fruits outside during a full moon could cause transformation from fruit to vampire fruit. Ethnologist Tatomir Vukanovi documented people's beliefs of this phenomenon:

> [T]his transformation occurs if these ground fruit have been kept for more than ten days: then the gathered pumpkins stir all by themselves and make a sound like "brrl, brrl, brrl!" and begin to shake themselves ... These pumpkins and melons go round the houses, stables, and rooms at night, all by themselves, and do harm to people. But it is thought that they cannot do great damage to folk, so people are not very afraid of this kind of vampire.

The Balkans' vampire watermelons

Guarding the Home

Many traditional methods of repelling vampires focused on the home. Thresholds and doorways were highly symbolic and believed to give more than just physical protection. In ancient Rome, the threshold was seen as the gateway between the dangerous outside world and the safe comfort of the house. Passing through a front door was almost a sacred act. Critic G. J. Bois notes that the door to a home marked "the boundary of the domestic sanctuary against external evil forces." Traditionally in folklore, evil creatures or spirits were only able to enter a house through a door or chimney.

Naturally, people tried to find ways to protect their homes. Romans would place **effigies** of gods at their entrance door. Even our modern tradition of carrying a new bride across the threshold of her new home is descended from these Roman beliefs. They believed that this stopped witches or bad luck from entering the home.

In vampire literature, thresholds and boundaries are important. Most vampires cannot enter a house without explicit permission. Sometimes access has to be gained by trickery or hypnotism. This reveals the theme of complicity hidden in most vampire tales. If vampires are evil creatures of darkness, then humans have a personal decision on whether to let that evil into their homes and perhaps their hearts. Once a person, willingly or unwillingly, makes the choice to allow evil, then evil may reenter at any time. This can be seen most strongly in vampire tales from highly religious societies.

The Soul of the Vampire

Do vampires have souls? Can they feel love, guilt, or shame? Where do they go when they meet their final death? Are they inherently good or evil? These questions have fascinated countless generations and are topics many modern-day folklorists have returned to time and again. The character of the vampire continues to be painted in more and more complex and **nuanced** ways. It has evolved from a mindless appetite on legs to a creature that wrestles with its place in the universe and its own religious beliefs. So why is a soul so important? Traditionally, it is humankind's most human feature. It supposedly gives humans a moral compass and permits a religious believer access to a life beyond death. Particularly in Christian literature, a person's soul can be lost to evil through accidental or deliberate immoral acts and decisions. Vampires are often believed to be soulless, having lost their souls at the moment of death. Proof of this is shown in their enjoyment of violence, hunting, and feeding on humans. However, they are also considered to be mostly human. If that is the case, can't vampires also experience human conflict and feeling? Most cultures believe that every person is born with a soul, and yet this does not prevent humans perpetrating acts of violence and cruelty similar to vampires. In fact, many modern literary vampires wrestle constantly with their "animal instincts" and are drawn to human love interests because of their moral goodness. Society's struggle with this question reveals much about our own battles with defining what it means to be human.

MOVING WITH THE TIMES

"Popular culture no longer craves archangels and new dawns. Pop culture traffics in vampires and deads of night."

Jᴀᴍᴇs Wᴏʟᴄᴏᴛᴛ

Each generation has used the figure of the vampire to reflect on and explore the issues of the era. Early history made the vampire a culprit for rampant disease and a cover for its lack of scientific knowledge. The Victorians and their contemporaries made the vampire a mask for a country's growing concerns over the breakdown of traditional family structures and religious beliefs. The twentieth century saw vampires take center stage on the silver screen and become objects that were both feared and fascinating. However, they were still symbols of evil—something for humanity to fight against.

Our modern times have allowed new technology and more acceptance for different ways of living to calm old fears around

Opposite: Brad Pitt (*right*) and Kirsten Dunst (*left*) star in the film adaptation of Anne Rice's *Interview with the Vampire*.

mortality and morality. Tracking vampires from the 1970s to today, we can see this evolution. The age-old concerns of death and evil have evolved into something far more nuanced. We do not fear sudden unexplainable death but rather the slow process of aging. Evil is no longer an external force that attacks from all sides but rather an internal part of ourselves that we can choose to fight or accept. Today's vampires ask us what it truly means to be human.

The Beautiful and the Damned

In 1976, author Anne Rice took the vampire world by storm with her novel *Interview with the Vampire*, the first book of her Vampire Chronicles series. Though it initially received mixed reviews from critics, it soon built up a cult following. The novel tells the story of a vampire named Louis through an interview he is giving to a young reporter. It charts his life from the moment he is made a vampire up to the present day. As Louis slowly comes to terms with his condition, he struggles between his new power and his old humanity. His hunger for blood forces him towards acts of violence that disgust his sensitive nature. Louis remains torn between his need for love and companionship and his self-loathing. Anne Rice had brought a new kind of vampire to a new generation.

Some critics have argued that in the 1970s and 1980s America saw an increase in people's distrust of authority. This was thought to coincide with new wealth created through stock market success on Wall Street. Many citizens had very little trust for the government after events such as the Vietnam War and the Watergate scandal. A small percentage of the population had become very wealthy and was seen by the rest of the population to be self-serving. These contrasting feelings of a population manifested in Anne Rice's vampires. Louis is **turned** by an old European vampire named Lestat, who soon shows himself to be without pity or mercy and believes himself above all ethical concerns. He is a figure of authority that Louis must reject in order to hold on to his last shred of humanity. His new vampire status gives him power over humans, and Louis must decide for himself the kind of person he wishes to be.

The New Rulebook

If the 1970s and 1980s were characterized by distrust and wealth, then the 1990s were a decade of power—specifically "Girl Power." Pop cultural icons such as the Spice Girls became popular because of their messages of female power and friendship. One other icon was Buffy Summers, otherwise known as Buffy the Vampire Slayer, a girl from the fictional town of Sunnyvale.

Buffy the Vampire Slayer was originally created as a movie by the writer Joss Whedon. After the movie's introduction in 1992, Whedon developed it into a popular TV show. Both the movie and the show follow teenager Buffy through high school and all of her encounters with the supernatural. On the outside, Buffy Summers looks like a typical teenager, though she is anything but. She is the "Chosen One," responsible for destroying evil on Earth, mostly through vampire hunting. Whedon designed Buffy as an expectation-subverting character. He said, "The idea for the film came from seeing too many blondes walking into dark alleyways and being killed. I wanted, just once, for her to fight back when the monster attacked."

Why should Whedon choose a vampire slayer as his heroine? According to scholar Bruce McClelland, "From the earliest

Kristy Swanson as Buffy Summers in the original *Buffy the Vampire Slayer* film

[times], the person assigned the task of identifying the otherwise unknowable source of disease or evil was given a high degree of authority." Buffy's position gives her power. Unlike past generations of films where young girls were usually the first to die, Buffy is a figure of strength and order. She makes decisions, leads a group of fellow crime fighters, and is both physically and mentally capable.

Buffy also dealt with more than female empowerment. It provided metaphors for high school students facing their day-to-day problems. As teenagers must adjust to intense emotions, body changes, and a new interest in relationships, so Buffy and her gang must adapt to new challenges. The show condensed these issues and put a recognizable face onto the problem: that of the ever-mutable vampire. What was revolutionary about the show was the use of emotions. Instead of being told that they were being controlled by their emotions, teenagers were shown characters that were able to channel their impulses into something powerful. Buffy used her anger to win fights where the odds were stacked against her. Her best friend, Willow, finds energy through her anguish to perform powerful spells. This message was confirmed by Buffy's other friend, Xander, in the final season: "Power is what you have, control is what you do with it."

Vampire Boyfriends

As time moves on, generational vampires continue to respond to each other. Our current generation has reacted to the past by making the vampire more humanlike. He—the vast majority of fictional vampires are male—has been tamed by his own victim. The nightgown-clad heroine is now being chased, not for food but

Kristen Stewart and Robert Pattinson play the star-crossed *Twilight* lovers, Bella and Edward.

for love. The latest incarnation of the vampire is the "supernatural boyfriend," a figure that is both a sensitive, complicated being and a status prize for the leading lady.

With the rise of books, films, and TV shows such as *Twilight*, *The Vampire Diaries*, and *True Blood*, vampires have become the new demigods—impossibly beautiful and immortal. The storylines often involve a seemingly normal teenage girl who is an outsider in her community meeting an equally angsty vampire who has conveniently been turned during his teenage years. She is drawn to him, and of course, he is intensely attracted to her. Gone are the days where jocks ruled high school hearts.

From their ancient beginnings to their seventeenth-century manifestations to today's representations, vampires have appeared in many forms and in many cultures. They began life, so to speak, as a way for humanity to explain and understand disease, death, and bloodlust. They have moved from unknowable gods to unthinking monsters to examples of human experience free from limits. Vampires change with the times, adapting themselves to new attitudes and fears with each new generation. It is unlikely we will ever lose them entirely because they are reflections of our inner selves.

Nina Dobrev and Ian Somerhalder play Elena Gilbert and Damon Salvatore in *The Vampire Diaries*.

Glossary

aristocracy A class of people with rank and privilege.

canon A body of rules or standards that are universally binding in a field of art or study.

crystallize To assume a definite or recognizable form.

derivative A word that is formed from another, similar word.

derive To create something from something else.

effigy A representation or image.

guile Crafty or artful deception.

impiety Lack of reverence for God or sacred things.

infidel An old word used to describe a person who does not accept a particular faith.

maul To injure by a rough beating.

multifaceted Having many aspects or phases.

nuanced Having subtle differences in expression or meaning.

obstruction Something that blocks or hinders movement.

paragon A model of excellence.

sentience Capacity for feeling or sensation.

spawned Gave birth to.

succubus A female demon who takes life energy from men.

suffragettes Female advocates of a woman's right to vote.

thwarted Prevented from accomplishing something.

trope A recurring literary device that uses a word in a not literal way.

turned Changed into a vampire.

wasting Gradual reduction of the strength of the body.

To Learn More About Vampires

Books

Day, William Patrick. *Vampire Legends in Contemporary American Culture: What Becomes a Legend Most*. Lexington, KY: University Press of Kentucky, 2014.

McLeod, Judyth A. *Vampires: A Bite-Sized History*. Sydney, Australia: Allen & Unwin, 2010.

Williamson, Milly. *The Lure of the Vampire: Gender, Fiction and Fandom from Bram Stoker to Buffy*. New York: Wallflower Press, 2005.

Website

Encyclopedia.com
www.encyclopedia.com/topic/Vampires.aspx
Learn more about the history and science behind vampirism.

Video

History of the Vampire
news.discovery.com/history/videos/history-history-of-vampires.htm
Watch to learn more of the evolution of the vampire in film and literature.

Bibliography

Auerbach, Nina. *Our Vampires, Ourselves.* Chicago: University of Chicago Press, 2012.

Bois, G. J. C. *Jersey Folklore & Superstitions Volume Two: A Comparative Study with the Traditions of the Gulf of St. Malo (the Channel Islands, Normandy & Brittany) with reference to World Mythologies.* Bloomington, IN: AuthorHouse, 2010.

Butler, Erik. *Metamorphoses of the Vampire in Literature and Film: Cultural Transformations in Europe, 1732–1933.* Rochester, NY: Camden House, 2010.

Byron, Glennis and Sharon Deans. "Teen Gothic." In *The Cambridge Companion to the Modern Gothic*, edited by Jerrold E. Hogle, 87–106. Cambridge, UK: Cambridge University Press, 2014.

Hirmer, Karen. "Female Empowerment: Buffy and her Heiresses in Control." In *Images of the Modern Vampire: The Hip and the Atavistic*, edited by Barbara Brodman and James E Doan, 71–84. Lanham, MD: Fairleigh Dickinson University Press, 2013.

Holte, James Craig. *Dracula in the Dark: The Dracula Film Adaptations.* Contributions to the Study of Science Fiction and Fantasy. Westport, CT: Greenwood Press, 1997.

Hurwitz, Siegmund. *Lilith the First Eve: Historical and Psychological Aspects of the Dark Feminine.* Translated by Gela Jacobson. Einsiedeln, Switzerland: Damon Verlag, 2007.

Kramer, Samuel. N. *Gilgamesh and the Huluppu-Tree: A Reconstructed Sumerian Text.* Assyriological Studies 10. Chicago: Oriental Institute of the University of Chicago, 1938.

Le Fanu, Joseph Sheridan. *Carmilla: A Critical Edition.* Edited by Kathleen Costello-Sullivan. Syracuse, NY: Syracuse University Press, 2013.

McClelland, Bruce. *Slayers and Their Vampires: A Cultural History of Killing the Dead.* Ann Arbor, MI: University of Michigan Press, 2006.

Pratchett, Terry. *Carpe Jugulum.* London: Transworld Books, 2008.

Scott, Keith. "Blood, Bodies, Books: Kim Newman and the Vampire as Cultural Text." In *The Modern Vampire and Human Identity*, edited by Deborah Mutch, 18–36. New York: Palgrave Macmillan, 2012.

Signorotti, Elizabeth. "Repossessing the Body: Transgressive Desire in 'Carmilla' and *Dracula*." *Criticism* 38 no. 4 (Fall 1996): 607–632.

Stoker, Bram. Dracula. World Signature Series. Germany: Uber Books, 2015.

Vukanovi, T. P. "The Vampire." *Journal of the Gypsy Lore Society* 36 (1957): 125–133.

Index

Page numbers in **boldface** are illustrations. Entries in **boldface** are glossary terms.

aristocracy, 32, 36, 42

Buffy the Vampire Slayer, 11, 25, 55–57, **56**

canon, 12
Carmilla, 12, 26, **26**, 36, 42
crystallize, 32

derivative, 13
derive, 13
Dracula (book), 12, 24–27, **30**, 31–37
Dracula (film), 37, **37**

effigy, 50

guile, 13

impiety, 36
infidel, 34–35
Interview with the Vampire, **52**, 54–55

Le Fanu, Joseph Sheridan, 12, 26, 36
Lilith, 19, **19**
Lilitu, **14**, 15–17

maul, 46
multifaceted, 10

Nosferatu, **24**, 37
nuanced, 51, 54

obstruction, 40

paragon, 10
Penanggalan, 11, 47–48, **47**

Sekhmet, **44**, 46
sentience, 26
spawned, 13, 32
Stoker, Bram, 12, 24, 26–27, **30**, 31–37
succubus, 19
suffragettes, 33

thwarted, 46
trope, 11, 23
turned, 55, 58
Twilight series, 7, **8**, 10–11, 25, **57**, 58

Vampire Diaries, The, 11, 25, 58, **59**
vampires
    appearance of, 9, 12, 19, 25, 32, 36, 41
    in European history, 19–21, 40
    in folklore and mythology, 10–13, 15–19, 21, 37, 45–48
    in literature, 12, 24–27, 31–37, 41–42
    in popular culture, 10–11, 25, 27, 54–58
    powers of, 13, 23–27, 32–33
    protecting against, **11**, 20–21, **28**, 29, 40, 49–50
    significance of, 10–11, 33, 39–43, 45–46, 53–58
Vlad the Impaler, 34–35, **34**

wasting, 47

About the Author

Katie Griffiths began a lifelong fascination with vampires during her childhood, where she devoured mythology from all around the world. She likes her vampires as she likes her coffee: strong, dark, and no sparkles. A native of England, she has returned home after spending two years teaching English in China. To learn more about her, visit her website: www.katiegriffiths.org.